HAL•LEONARD

Classical

PLAY-ALONG™

Volume 19

Johannes BRAHMS

(1833-1897)

Clarinet Sonata in F Minor, Op. 120, No. 1

The Hal Leonard Classical Play-Along™ series allows you to work through great classical works systematically and at any tempo with accompaniment.

Tracks 2-5 on the CD demonstrate the concert version of each movement. After tuning your instrument to Track 1 you can begin practicing the piece. Using the Amazing Slow-Downer technology included on the CD, you can adjust the recording to any tempo you like without altering the pitch. (Note that when using Amazing Slow-Downer, the CD will stop after each track instead of playing continuously.)

- Track No. ☐ 1 – tuning notes
- Track numbers in circles ◯ – concert version
- Track numbers in diamonds ◆ – play-along version

CONCERT VERSION

Nandor Götz, Clarinet

Hilda Hernadi, Piano

ISBN 978-1-4234-8893-4

HAL•LEONARD®
CORPORATION

7777 W. BLUEMOUND RD. P.O. BOX 13819 MILWAUKEE, WI 53213

In Australia Contact:
Hal Leonard Australia Pty. Ltd.
4 Lentara Court
Cheltenham, Victoria, 3192 Australia
Email: ausadmin@halleonard.com.au

Visit Hal Leonard Online at
www.halleonard.com

SONATA Op. 120 No. 1

for Clarinet in F Minor

Johannes Brahms (1833–1897)

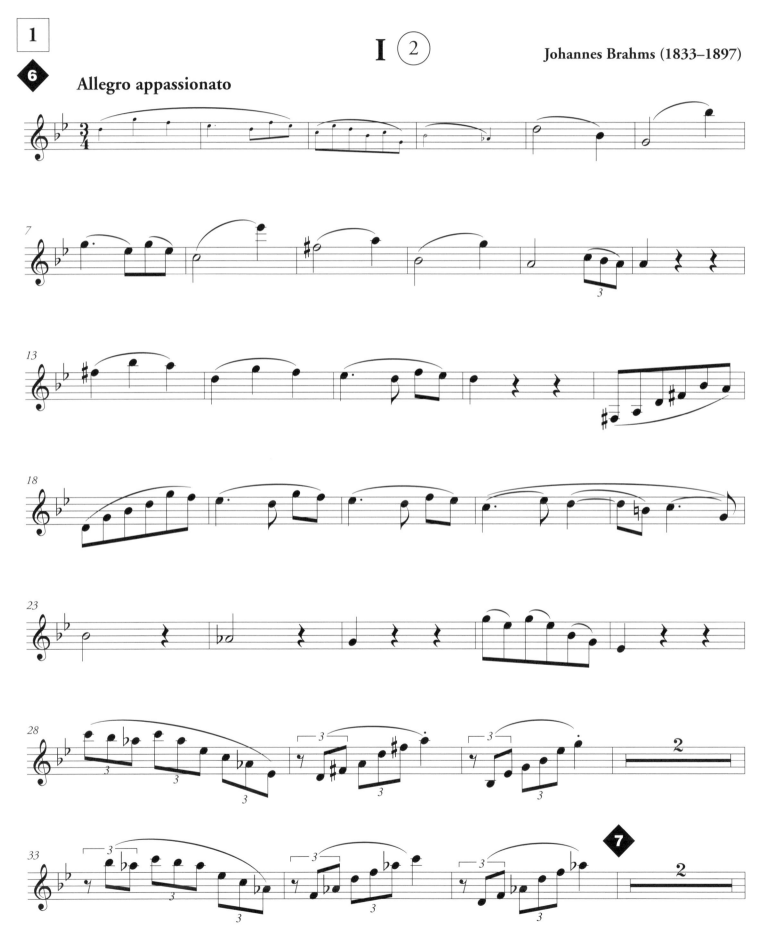

Sostenuto ed espressivo

II ③

12 **Andante un poco Adagio**

14

Allegretto grazioso

15

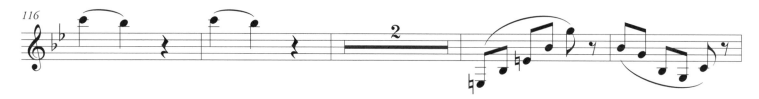

IV ⑤

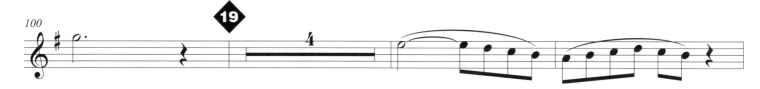

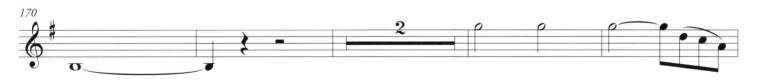